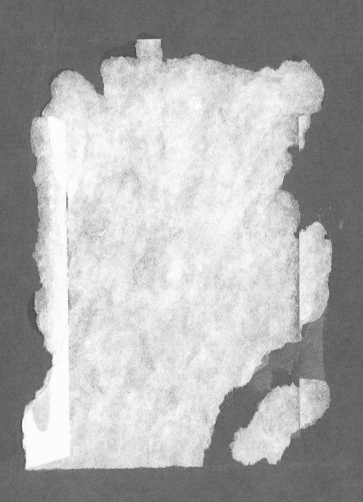

Over the River
and Through the Wood

Over the River

and Through the Wood

Lydia Maria Child
illustrated by Iris Van Rynbach

LITTLE, BROWN AND COMPANY
Boston Toronto London

First edition

The text for this book was originally entitled "A Boy's Thanksgiving
Day," first published in 1844 in the second volume of *Flowers for
Children* by Lydia Maria Child (C.S. Francis & Co., NY).

Library of Congress Cataloging-in-Publication Data

Child, Lydia Maria Francis, 1802–1880.
    [Boy's Thanksgiving Day]
    Thanksgiving Day/by Lydia Maria Child; illustrated by Iris Van
Rynbach. — 1st ed.
        p.   cm.
    Text originally published in v. 2 of the author's Flowers for
children, 1844, under title: A boy's Thanksgiving Day.
    Summary: An illustrated version of the well-known text describing
the joys of a Thanksgiving visit to grandmother's house.
    [1. Thanksgiving Day — Poetry.   2. Songs.]   I. Van Rynbach, Iris.
ill.   II. Title.
PZ8.3.C4335TH 1989
811'.2 — dc19   88-4712
                                                                        CIP
                                                                         AC

10 9 8 7 6 5 4 3

WOR

Published simultaneously in Canada
by Little, Brown & Company (Canada) Limited

Printed in the United States of America

Illustrations done in watercolor and pen and ink on Arches watercolor paper

Musical arrangement for "Over the River
and Through the Wood"
by Frederich Jodry

For Vicki Martin Guertin

and

Karen Klockner

Over the river and through the wood,
To grandfather's house we go;

The horse knows the way
To carry the sleigh
Through the white and drifted snow.

Over the river and through the wood —
Oh, how the wind does blow!

It stings the toes
And bites the nose,
As over the ground we go.

Over the river and through the wood,
To have a first-rate play.
Hear the bells ring,
"Ting-a-ling-ding!"
Hurrah for Thanksgiving Day!

Over the river and through the wood
Trot fast, my dapple-gray!
Spring over the ground,
Like a hunting-hound!
For this is Thanksgiving Day.

Over the river and through the wood,
 And straight through the barn-yard gate.

We seem to go
Extremely slow, —
It is so hard to wait!

Over the river and through the wood —
Now grandmother's cap I spy!

Hurrah for the fun!

Is the pudding done?

Hurrah for the pumpkin-pie!

Over the River
and Through the Wood

words by Lydia Maria Child

musical arrangement by Frederich Jodry

Over the river and through the wood, to grandfather's house we go; the horse knows the way to carry the sleigh through the

2. Over the river and through
   the wood,
   To have a first-rate play.
   Hear the bells ring,
   "Ting-a-ling-ding!"
   Hurrah for Thanksgiving Day!

Over the river and through
the wood
Trot fast, my dapple-gray!
Spring over the ground,
Like a hunting-hound!
For this is Thanksgiving Day.

white and drifted snow. Over the river and

through the wood — oh, how the wind does blow! It

stings the toes and bites the nose, as over the ground we go.

3. Over the river and through
   the wood,
   And straight through the
   barn-yard gate
   We seem to go
   Extremely slow, —
   It is so hard to wait!

Over the river and through
the wood —
Now grandmother's cap I spy!
Hurrah for the fun!
Is the pudding done?
Hurrah for the pumpkin-pie!